INCREDIBLE DEVICES!

The Math of Technology

Written by Izzi Howell

WORLD BOOK

www.worldbook.com

Co-published by agreement between Shi Tu Hui and World Book, Inc.

Shi Tu Hui
Room 1807, Block 1,
#3 West Dawang Road
Chaoyang District, Beijing 100025
P.R. China

World Book, Inc.
180 North LaSalle Street
Suite 900
Chicago, Illinois 60601
USA

© 2026. All rights reserved. This volume may not be reproduced in whole or in part in any form without prior written permission from the publisher.

WORLD BOOK and the GLOBE DEVICE are registered trademarks or trademarks of World Book, Inc.

Library of Congress Control Number: 2025942229

Aha! Academy: Math
ISBN: 978-0-7166-7377-4 (set, hardcover)

Incredible Devices! The Math of Technology
ISBN: 978-0-7166-7385-9 (hard cover)
ISBN: 978-0-7166-7448-1 (e-book)
ISBN: 978-0-7166-7438-2 (soft cover)

Staff

Editorial

Vice President
Tom Evans

Editorial Project Coordinator
Kaile Kilner

Senior Curriculum Designer
Caroline Davidson

Curriculum Designer
Mikayla Kightlinger

Proofreader
Nathalie Strassheim

Indexer
Nathaniel Lindstrom

Graphics and Design

Senior Visual
Communications Designer
Melanie Bender

Designer
Shannon Hagman

Written by Izzi Howell

Developed with World Book by The Dream Team

Acknowledgments

The publishers gratefully acknowledge the following sources for photography. All illustrations were prepared by WORLD BOOK unless otherwise noted.

Cover: aapsky/Shutterstock; Hodoimg/Shutterstock; IM Imagery/Shutterstock; MikeDotta/Shutterstock; Volodymyr TVERDOKHLIB/Shutterstock

© dpa picture alliance/Alamy 39; © ep stock/Alamy 40; Konrad Jacobs, Erlangen (licensed under CC BY-SA 2.0 DE) 20; NASA 30, 31, 32, 33, 34, 35, 45; © Phanie - Sipa Press/Alamy 36; The Picture Art Collection/Alamy 10; © Shutterstock 3, 4, 5, 6, 7, 8, 9, 10, 11, 12, 13, 14, 15, 16, 17, 18, 19, 20, 21, 22, 23, 24, 25, 26, 27, 28, 29, 31, 35, 36, 37, 38, 39, 40, 41, 42, 43, 44, 46, 47, 48; © World History Archive/Alamy 27; © Zuma Press, Inc./Alamy 43

There is a glossary of terms on page 48. Terms defined in the glossary are in type that looks like *this* on their first appearance on any spread (two facing pages).

Contents

Introduction 4

① Gadgets and games 6
    Get in the game! 8
    Computers: past and present 10
    Staying in touch 12
    Smart living 14

② Transportation and infrastructure 16
    Out and about 18
    By air and sea 20
    Green energy structures 22
    Amazing infrastructure 24

③ Space exploration 26
    Staring into space 28
    Spacecraft design 30
    Humankind on the moon 32
    Mission to Mars 34

④ Into the future 36
    Robotic friends 38
    Medical math 40
    Faster, higher, farther 42

Design and make a space parachute 44
Index 46
Glossary 48

Introduction

Technology is everywhere. It's so much a part of our everyday lives that most of the time, we don't even notice that we're using it. But stop for a moment and think about the tech that you use on a daily basis— do you realize how much of it starts with math?

The truth is that smart scientists, amazing inventors, and ingenious engineers wouldn't get anywhere without math. The bike you ride, the bridge you bicycle across, the messaging app you use, the video game you can't tear yourself away from … none of these things would exist without math.

The mechanics of a bike, such as its design and gear ratios, are all calculated with math.

Let's take a closer look at the multitude of ways that math keeps the modern world moving!

Math gets to work every time you pick up your tablet.

1
GADGETS AND GAMES

You may not know it, but every time you use one of these devices you're activating and interacting with some pretty complex math! To begin with, most tech is driven by algorithms—sets of rules that have to be followed to solve a problem or complete a task.

What would you do without your computer, your phone, your TV, your smart speaker?

Think about how you make a piece of buttered toast:

Take a slice of bread.

Put it in the toaster.

Turn the toaster on.

When it pops up, take it out of the toaster.

Unwrap the butter.

Use a knife to spread butter on the toast.

Eat the buttered toast.

You have to do things in the right order and in the right way. For example, it wouldn't work if you spread the butter before you put the bread in the toaster. Algorithms are the same. They are codes that provide precise information about what, how, when, and where.

But that's just the start. From *algebra* to *equations*, *geometry* to *probability*, *calculus* to *logic*, mathematical processes power every gadget! Let's take a look inside some everyday devices to see how math makes them work.

What's going on in there?!

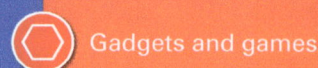
Gadgets and games

Get in the game!

Algorithms control your character or your enemies in a game by giving them rules to follow. These rules decide how the characters can move, react, and interact in any given situation.

The fantastic 3D graphics that bring a game to life are all about *geometry*. This creates light, shade, and perspective. Geometry also defines where you see objects and how you move around them.

Just about every aspect of video gameplay is made possible by math.

At a basic level, scores, timings, and progress in the game all rely on basic math. But there's more!

Where objects in a game appear and how they move are ruled by transformations:
- Translation moves a shape without changing its size or orientation.
- Rotation spins a shape around a fixed point, or axis.
- Reflection flips a shape over a line to create a mirror image of it.
- Scaling makes an object bigger or smaller, but keeps its shape in the same proportions.

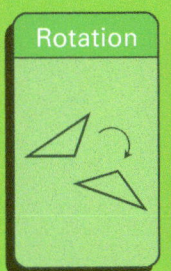

You've probably figured out which route through a game gets you the most bonuses. That involves *optimization* and game theory. Game designers use these ideas to keep things challenging!

Optimize your gameplay—which route gains the most coins?

DID YOU KNOW?

Game theory is a type of math that describes how decisions should be made. It ranks outcomes from different strategies and choices to decide which one is best.

Gadgets and games

Computers: past and present

In 1821, English mathematician Charles Babbage designed a machine that could compute tables of numbers. But this first computer was never actually built—the technology at the time wasn't advanced enough!

This is a plan for an algorithm for Babbage's "Analytical Engine."

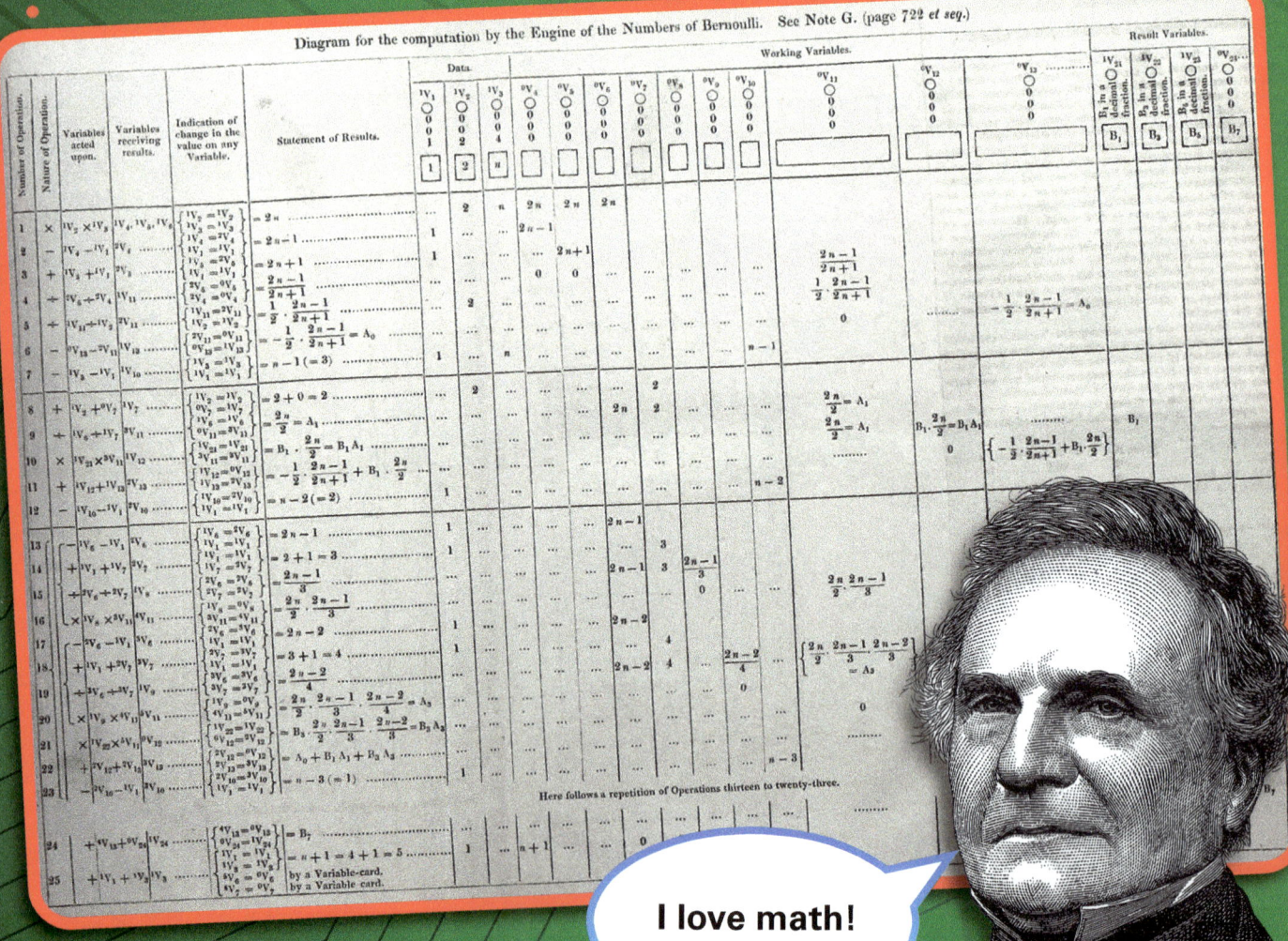

I love math!

You simply can't separate computers from math. After all, computers are machines that *compute*—they figure things out using mathematical processes.

In the twentieth century, Alan Turing's mathematical computation theory showed that machines could solve problems by following step-by-step instructions. He also invented the Turing test to determine whether a machine can show human intelligence.

ReCAPTCHA are tests you do to prove that you are a human when you visit a website. They are a type of modern Turing test.

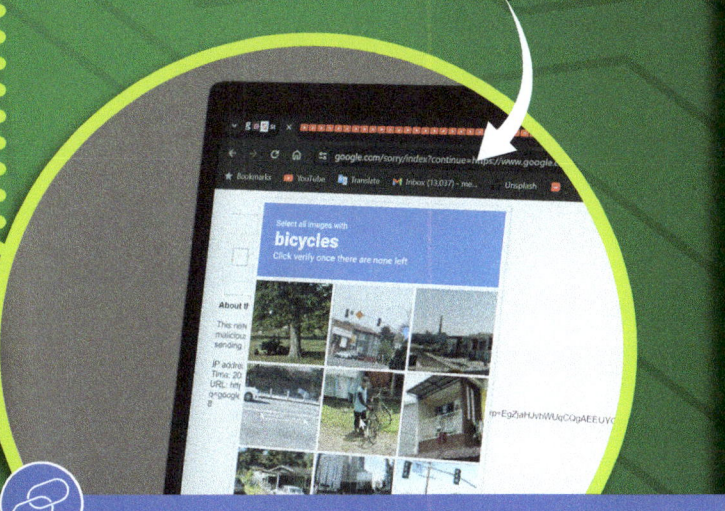

Math organizes the internet. For example, Google uses an algorithm called PageRank to sort web pages into search results. It does this by counting the number of links to a page and how good they are. It then calculates a website's importance.

Computers are also good at making predictions, thanks to differential *equations.* These show how something changes over time—in what ways and how fast. This helps scientists predict all kinds of things, from population growth to climate change.

CURIOUS CONNECTIONS
COMPUTER SCIENCE

Binary math—the numbers 0 and 1—underpins all computer coding. These numbers combine to represent data. For example, computers use these numbers to encode email data, process it through servers, and deliver the message to somebody as normal text.

Gadgets and games

Staying in **touch**

Hello? Hello?

When you make a call, it sends a digital version of what you say as an electronic signal. Error-correction math detects and fixes transmission errors in that signal by adding extra data. This ensures that the person you're talking to hears you loud and clear!

You want your text messages to be secure, so messaging apps like WhatsApp generate unique number keys for each user. These keys *encrypt* messages, so that only the person who is supposed to get the message can decode them. Even WhatsApp can't read the messages.

WHATSAPP   now
Message
Name
2 more notifications

The way we communicate has changed dramatically in the past few decades.

Now we have tech that allows us to stay in touch 24-7. What part does math play in that?

Isn't it spooky how social media apps seem to read your mind? They fill your feed with posts, videos, and ads tailored to your interests. They can do this because their algorithms analyze your clicks and interactions to figure out what you like.

CAREER CORNER

Social media is a mine of information. Get to grips with algorithms and *statistics,* and you can have a career as a data engineer. You'll find new ways to collect, store, and transform all that data, so it can be accessed and analyzed by interested organizations.

⬣ Gadgets and games

Smart living

Smart assistants like Siri and Alexa use *statistics,* collecting and analyzing numerical data. They record sound waves from your voice and turn them into code. Software analyzes that code and identifies particular words and speech patterns to figure out what you're asking.

How can I help you?

In the kitchen, your smart refrigerator calculates weights, quantities, and expiration dates using sensors or barcode scanners. It also uses statistics to predict when food items will run out.

Every new gadget adds another "smart" dimension to our daily lives. Let's take a tour around a smart home and see how math makes it all possible.

Smart thermostats are extra clever! They use *machine learning* algorithms to remember what your perfect temperature is, when you like to crank up the heating, and when you prefer to keep cool.

Deep learning **algorithms are also used in home security systems.** They help monitor what's going on in real time, and respond to potential threats.

TECH TIME

The Internet of Things is the name given to everyday objects that are all linked via the internet. This allows the devices to send and receive data, and interact with each other. They can also be controlled remotely for smarter living!

TRANSPORTATION AND INFRASTRUCTURE

When you step outside your front door, bikes, cars, buses, trains, and all kinds of other technology can transport you from A to B. Designing and constructing these vehicles involves math.

Math powers more than just the tech in our homes and pockets. It also plays a big part in the wider world.

Once they're built, vehicles need infrastructure to get around. That means planning and building things like bridges, tunnels, roads, and railroads. And those things need complicated traffic control technology. None of these could exist without math.

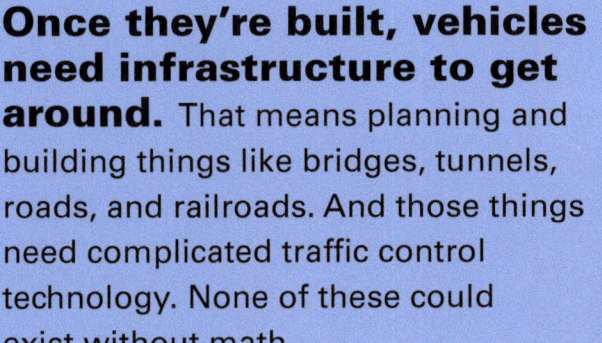

An increasingly important part of modern infrastructure is the way that we get our energy—for example, electrical grids and such renewable sources as wind, water, and the sun. Experts use math to get the most out of these resources.

So, let's take a trip to see some different types of transportation and structures, designed and built by the best mathematical minds!

Transportation and infrastructure

Out and about

Car manufacturers use math *formulas* from start to finish:

- to work out a car's *volume*—how big it should be
- to figure out the best shape and surface area, so that air flows over it smoothly
- to calculate its weight and its top speed.

Computers make super-precise measurements—down to the size of an atom—to ensure that every car is perfect.

Remember how *optimization* helps players make the best decisions when gaming (page 9)? It helps in real life, too. Optimization in traffic flow management systems, such as traffic lights, keeps everyone safe on the roads.

From smart roads to GPS to vehicle design, math drives all different types of travel technology.

GPS is an amazing system of satellites and receivers that send and receive signals at about the speed of light (almost 186,000 miles per second, or 300,000 kilometers per second). It uses trilateration to locate a vehicle based on how far away it is from three other points.

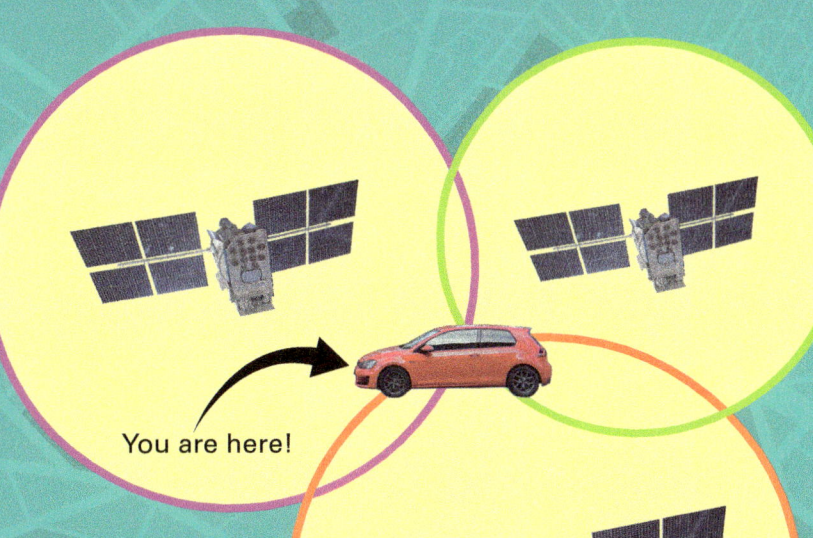

You are here!

Like cars, math is used to design trains, but it also controls the *way* that trains run. Planning routes, creating timetables, even deciding how much to charge passengers—they're all calculated with math!

CAREER CORNER

An automotive engineer designs, builds, and tests cars. These awesome engineers turn inventive ideas into smart, *streamlined* machines while solving math puzzles to make vehicles safe, efficient, and fun to drive!

Transportation and infrastructure

By air and sea

During World War II (1939-1945), **Abraham Wald** (1902–1950) applied math to military problems. By analyzing bullet holes on planes that got back safely, he figured out which other parts of the planes needed reinforcing. Wald's math saved many lives.

Aeronautical engineers use *equations* to calculate aerodynamics—the way that things move through the air. For example:

lift = ½ × air density × wing area × lift coefficient × speed squared

The equation basically means that the faster a plane travels and the bigger its wings, the greater the amount of lift!

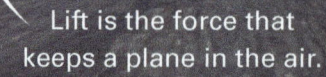
Lift is the force that keeps a plane in the air.

Other kinds of travel rely on math, too. Different types of math skills are needed to design the most efficient ships and planes and to control them safely.

***Trigonometry* skills are essential for pilots of both planes and ships,** because trigonometry is used to understand *vectors.* Vectors tell you something's magnitude (size) and direction—and that's important for making sure you don't get too close to another plane or ship!

Have you ever wondered how boats float? That can be explained by math, too! Archimedes's mathematical principle showed that something will float if the upward push—buoyancy—is strong enough to balance its *mass* (the downward pull of gravity).

gravity

buoyancy

21

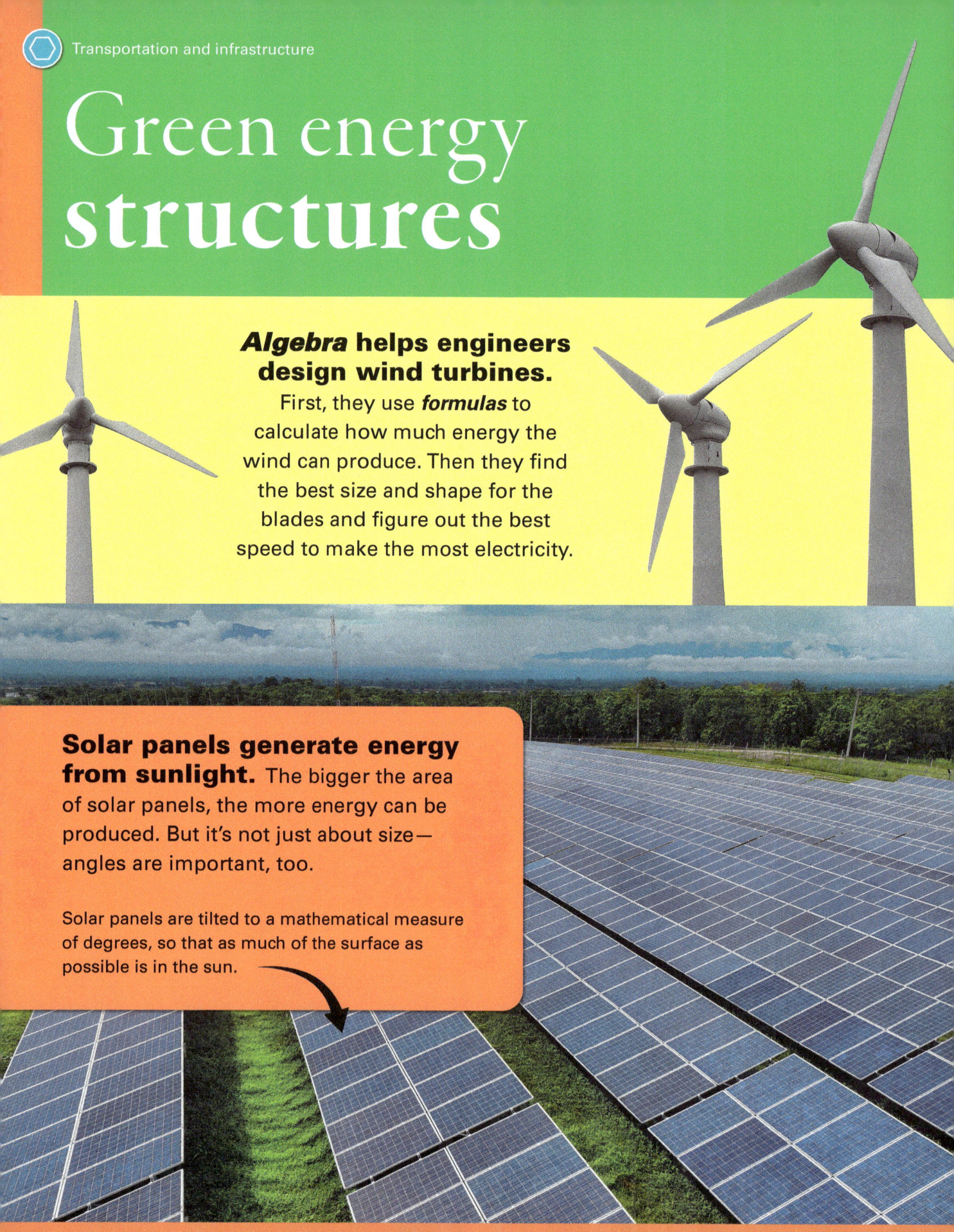

Transportation and infrastructure

Green energy structures

Algebra helps engineers design wind turbines. First, they use *formulas* to calculate how much energy the wind can produce. Then they find the best size and shape for the blades and figure out the best speed to make the most electricity.

Solar panels generate energy from sunlight. The bigger the area of solar panels, the more energy can be produced. But it's not just about size—angles are important, too.

Solar panels are tilted to a mathematical measure of degrees, so that as much of the surface as possible is in the sun.

About 30 percent of the world's electricity comes from renewable resources, such as wind, water, and solar power. These sources are all harnessed by incredible technology.

The efficiency of hydroelectric dams is calculated using the *equation* PE = mgh.

PE = potential energy
m = **mass**
g = gravity
h = height

So, the higher the water in a dam is, and the heavier it is, the more energy it has when it is about to fall.

DID YOU KNOW?

On the outside of the tallest building in the world, the Burj Khalifa in Dubai, 24,348 panels reflect the light and heat of the sun. This energy-saving design reduces the amount of air conditioning needed to cool things down inside.

Be cool!

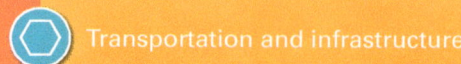
Transportation and infrastructure

Amazing infrastructure

Bridges and tunnels are all about *geometry*. Civil engineers have to figure out the best size, shape, angles, and dimensions to make the bridge or tunnel strong, safe, and efficient.

Engineers use math to make sure that all the pieces of a bridge fit together perfectly.

Infrastructure is all the things that a village, town, region, or country needs to function properly. You probably don't think about it, but you'd soon notice if it stopped working!

Mathematical modeling means using *equations* and *formulas* to create a kind of plan, or blueprint. It helps engineers predict how a structure will handle weight, high winds, or even things like earthquakes.

By studying how and where cracks appear in such infrastructure as bridges, tunnels, dams, and roads, experts can calculate which parts are taking the most stress. They can reinforce these areas and *optimize* the infrastructure.

Ancient Greek mathematician **Pythagoras** (570?–490 B.C.) changed the world with his theorem. He realized that in a right-angled triangle, the square of the hypotenuse (the longest side) is equal to the total of the squares of the two shorter sides: $a^2 + b^2 = c^2$. Engineers use this equation to calculate the height, length, angles, and loads that buildings and bridges need.

Chapter 3
SPACE EXPLORATION

Ancient astronomers used math to develop models to explain how things in space moved. From there, they began to predict such astronomical events as eclipses and how often comets would pass by.

Ancient astronomers didn't always get things right, but their experiments started unraveling the mysteries of space.

Have you ever looked up at the night sky and wondered how far away the moon is? How long it would take to get to Neptune? How many stars there are?

Space has fascinated humans for thousands of years. And right from the start, people realized that astronomy and math were closely linked.

I wonder how big Saturn's rings are?

Have you marveled at videos of the moon landing or a rocket launch and wondered how we can build spacecraft that can break free of Earth's gravity ... and then somehow land safely on other worlds?

Well, prepare yourself for a journey of discovery, and see how math provides the answers to all these questions.

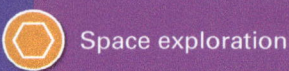
Space exploration

Staring into space

Modern telescopes are much more powerful. They work with cameras that record lots of numbers, including how much light different objects are emitting and what type of light it is. Experts interpret these numbers to learn about space bodies.

Telescopes have even helped us figure out roughly how old the universe itself is: 13.7 billion years. In scientific notation—the way scientists write math—that's 1.37×10^{10}.

Italian astronomer Galileo Galilei designed one of the earliest telescopes in 1609. This incredible instrument magnified objects in space by up to 20 times. But that was just the beginning!

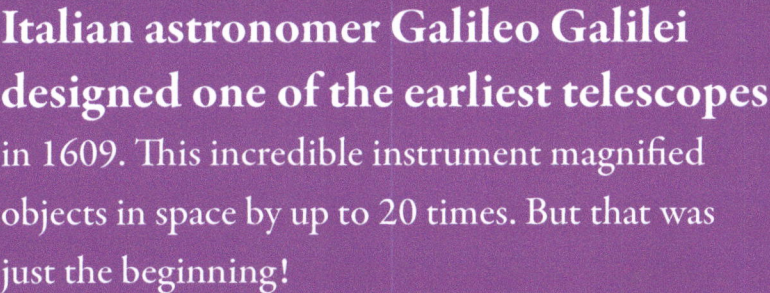

Galileo's telescope gave humans the first real glimpse of the moon's crater-covered surface.

Astronomers also use math to figure out the distances between objects in space. They send radio waves to the object, then they measure how long it takes for the waves to bounce back. Radio waves travel at the speed of light, so scientists multiply the time by the speed to find the distance.

DID YOU KNOW?

The fact that Earth's tiny moon completely blocks the giant sun during a solar eclipse is a mathematical coincidence! The moon is about 400 times smaller than the sun, but it's also about 400 times closer to Earth. So, from where we stand, they look the same size.

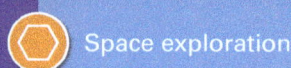

Space exploration

Spacecraft design

It's important to know how much fuel a spacecraft will need to reach its destination—and maybe come back again. Engineers balance the weight of the fuel, of the rocket itself, and of the *payload* to make sure there's enough fuel for the journey without overloading it.

They also need to calculate escape velocity—the speed a rocket needs to be traveling to break free of a planet's gravitational pull. The *formula* for escape velocity is $v = \sqrt{\frac{2GM}{r}}$, where:

> v = escape velocity
> G = gravitational constant of planet
> M = *mass* of planet
> r = *radius* of planet

We escaped!

Escape velocity from Earth works out to about 36,700 feet per second, or 11,186 meters per second!

Everything about designing and building a spacecraft is carefully calculated. One tiny error in the numbers could mean a countdown to disaster!

Orbital mechanics is a clever combination of physics and math. It uses the laws of motion and gravity to control how objects move in space. For example, smart scientists use orbital mechanics to figure out where to place satellites.

CAREER CORNER

If you think you'd have a talent for solving space puzzles, why not become a mathematical modeler for NASA? You'd create computer models that predict how rockets fly, planets move, and spacecraft survive to make sure that every space mission is successful!

Space exploration

Humankind on the moon

Some of the math that eventually landed the Apollo astronauts on the moon hadn't even been invented when NASA first worked on the mission! There were so many *variables* that they needed a whole new set of math *equations* to figure out the spacecraft's position and *trajectory*.

The Schmidt-Kalman filter combined estimated data with predictions based on the spacecraft's last known position and speed. The process was continually repeated to improve the accuracy of the data over time. This math is still used today to make sure that planes land on time!

On July 20, 1969, **Neil Armstrong and Buzz Aldrin** became the first humans to set foot on the moon. But how did they get there? It took years of research and planning by scientists, engineers, and mathematicians.

The International System of metric units (SI) was standard in computing. However, the astronauts were used to using imperial units of measurement. So, the computer on board calculated things in SI units, but converted them to imperial to display on screen!

JoAnn Morgan (1940-   ) joined NASA not long after it was established. She quickly made a name for herself as a Measurement and Instrumentation Engineer. Morgan was the Instrumentation Controller on Apollo 11—and the only woman in the control room at launch.

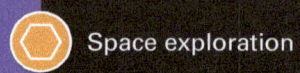
Space exploration

Mission to **Mars**

To safely land the Perseverence rover, scientists used orbital mechanics (see page 31) to figure out where it would enter Mars's atmosphere. They also had to calculate the speed, angle, and timing of its descent to make sure it landed safely—and in the right place!

Since 1997, six rovers have been sent to Mars. Two are currently still working—Curiosity (pictured) and Perseverance.

There have been lots of unmanned missions to Mars, but the most famous are the Mars rovers. These robotic vehicles land on Mars and send information about it back to Earth.

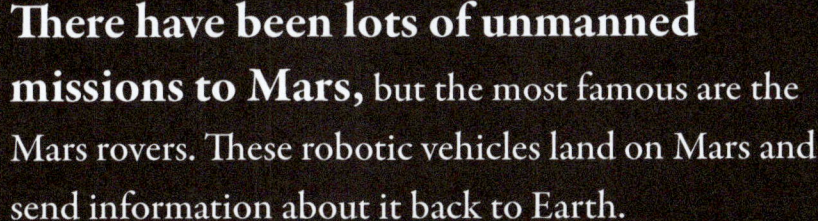

The rovers themselves are math wizards! They can:
- measure distances to map Mars's surface and avoid obstacles when moving around
- calculate how much heat they are absorbing and control their temperature
- measure the size, weight, and chemical makeup of rock and soil samples
- calculate the time it takes for messages to travel between Mars and Earth.

Selfie time!

TECH TIME

The Mars helicopter, Ingenuity, works thanks to the mathematical figure pi (π). Pi measures circles. Scientists used the *formula* $2\pi r$, where r is the *radius* of the helicopter blade, to find out how far the blade moved in one full spin. From there, they could calculate how fast the blades had to spin to fly in Mars's thin atmosphere.

④ INTO THE FUTURE

In the past few years, AI (artificial intelligence) has become a hot topic. It's revolutionizing our lives, and at times it can seem like magic. But at the heart of all AI is math—processes and ideas that help machines behave more like humans.

Math and technology are undoubtedly changing lives in hundreds of different ways, but they're also working together to *save* lives. Medicine is one of the most important areas where new technology is starting to make a big difference.

Robotic surgery is already happening in a hospital near you!

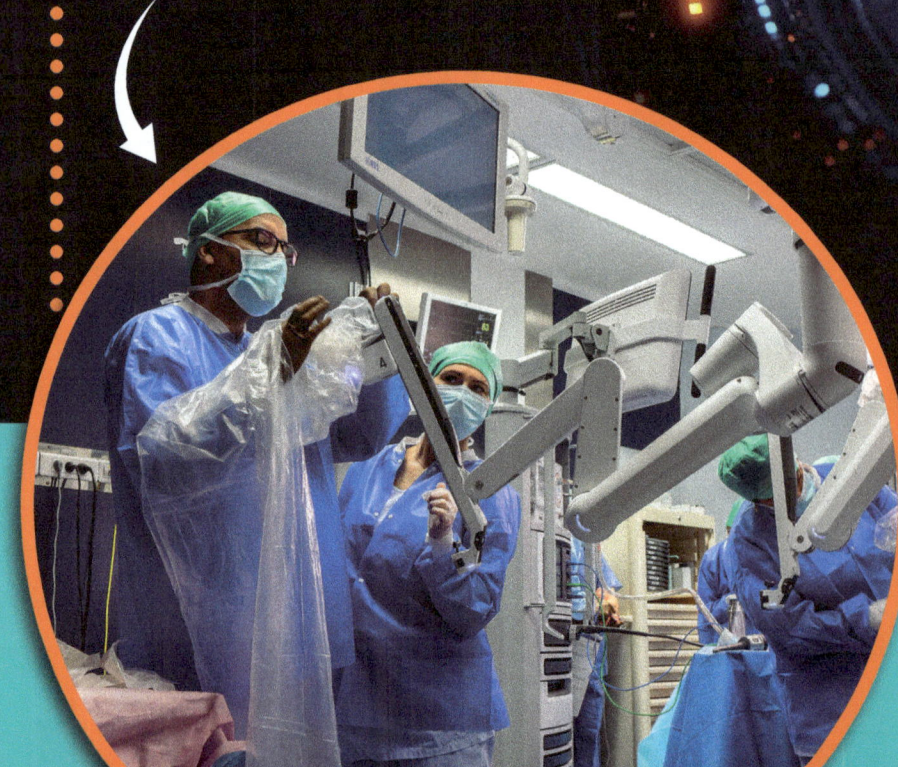

Scientists, engineers, and inventors are coming up with new math-driven technologies all the time. These are reshaping how we see the world and pushing the boundaries of what we can do.

Technology is also making life more fun!

And it's not just about coming up with new, more realistic games or other things online. Out in the real world, advances in tech are helping us keep fit, share ideas, find new hobbies, and set ourselves new challenges.

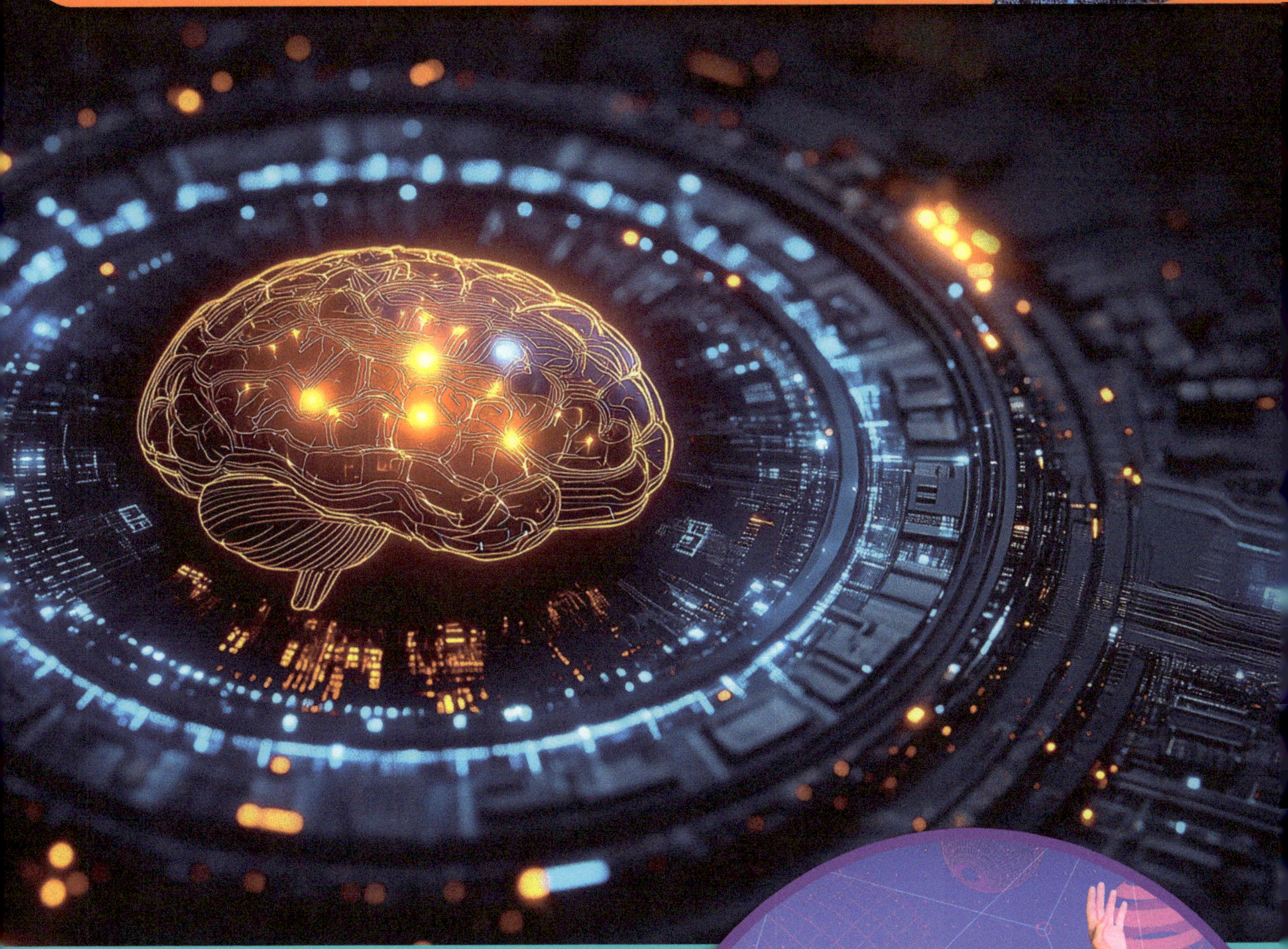

If you're ready to get a glimpse of the future, turn the page to see how math is influencing the technology of tomorrow.

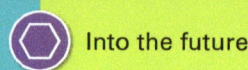

Into the future

Robotic friends

Kinematics is a type of math that deals with how things move, such as their speed and direction. Kinematics plays an important part in a robot's "brain."

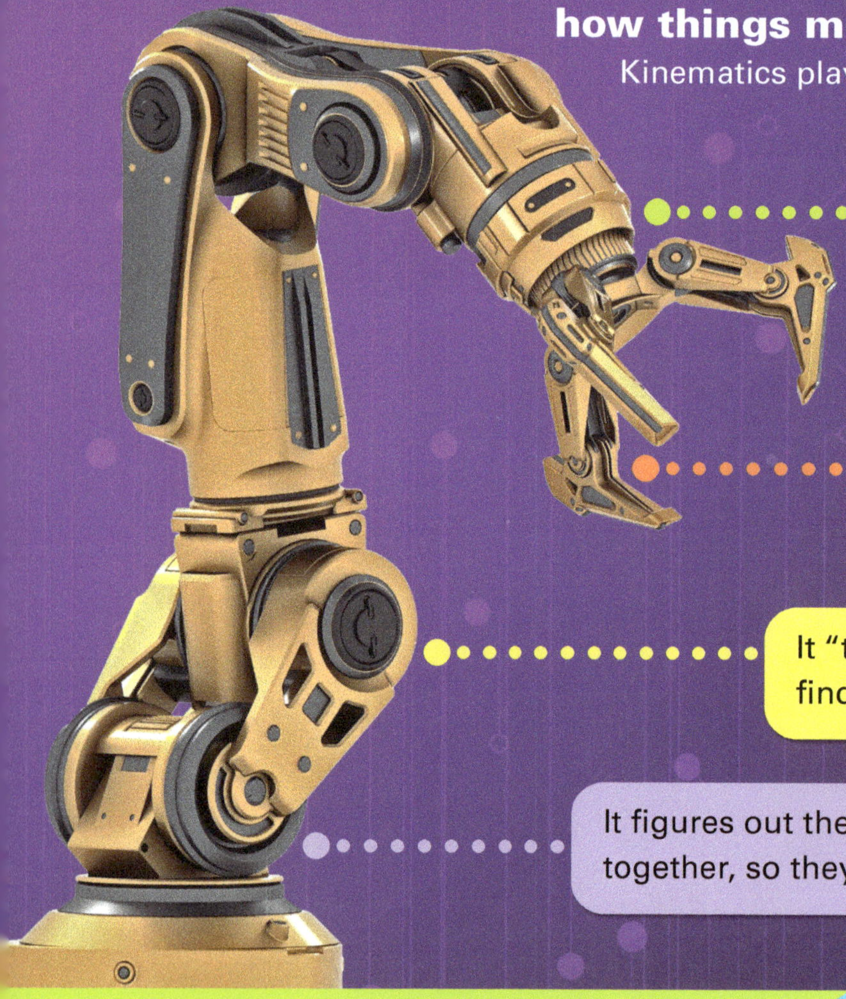

Kinematic math figures out how much each "joint" needs to bend or rotate to perform a task.

It calculates where the "hand" will end up based on joint movements.

It "thinks ahead," a little like finding out directions.

It figures out the best way to move all the parts together, so they perform a task smoothly.

***Algebra* helps robots make decisions**—such as choosing the best route around a room—and solve problems. For example, algebra helps a robot adjust to changes in its environment, like avoiding obstacles or dealing with a low battery!

Where do you think you're going?

The science of robotics has been around for many years. But with advances in AI and algorithms, engineers are now finding new and ingenious ways of putting robots to work!

Hi!

TECH TIME

Ameca is one of the most realistic humanoid robots ever invented. Thanks to advanced AI algorithms and *machine learning,* Ameca displays realistic facial expressions, can hold a conversation, and can learn in a humanlike way.

Advanced robots are always gathering and analyzing data and *statistics*. This brainy activity helps a robot track its own progress and learn from its successes and failures.

Into the future

Medical **math**

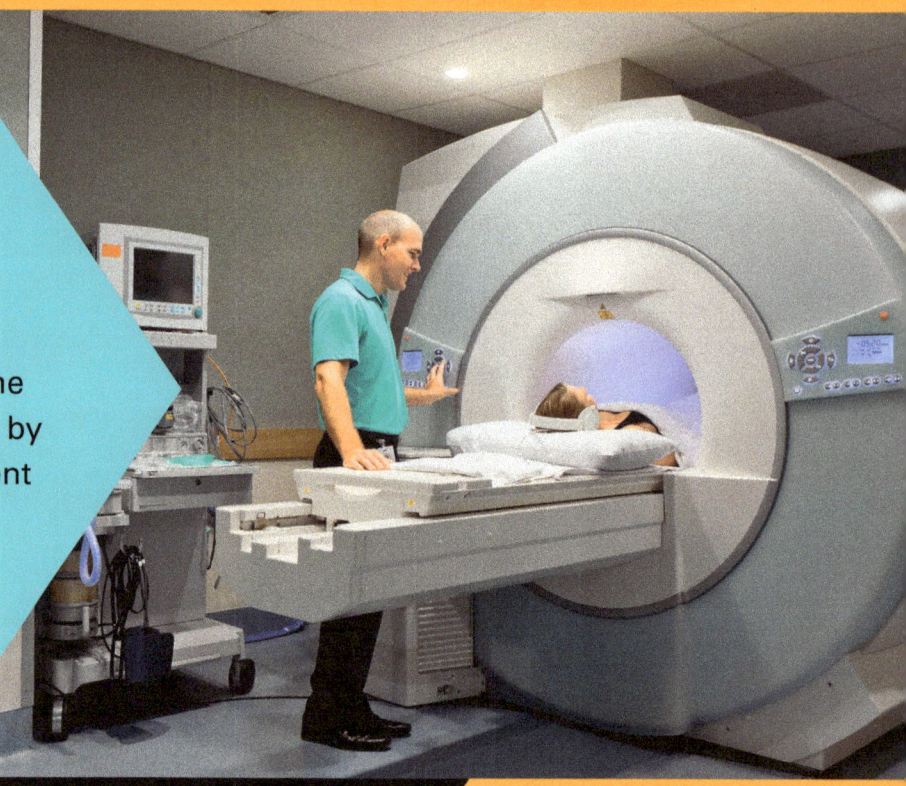

Today, math-powered tech is essential in diagnosing, treating, and curing disease. CT machines create pictures of the inside of your body. They do this by figuring out the density of different tissues, taking 2D images and reconstructing them in 3D.

MRI machines scan the body to collect data. But a math process called Fourier transform is needed to make sense of the data. This basically breaks down signals from the machine into smaller parts—like identifying all the individual ingredients in a complicated recipe!

You've probably experienced firsthand how math applies to medicine. Temperature, blood pressure, pulse rate—health is all about numbers!

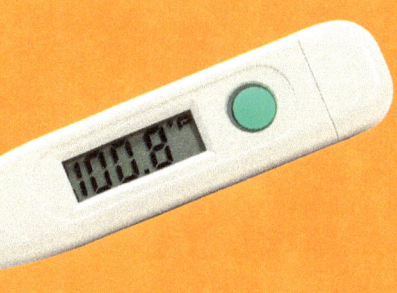

During the COVID-19 pandemic, math was used to calculate infection rates and analyze hospital data. Math could also be seen in the "R number." An R greater than 1 meant that the virus was spreading quickly. It was used to predict and map where the virus was heading.

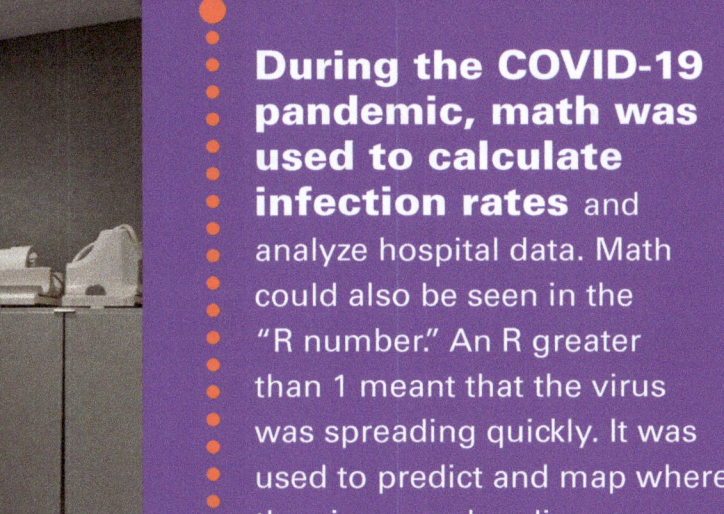

Can't catch me!

CURIOUS CONNECTIONS

BIOLOGY Bioengineering works by applying math and engineering ideas to solve problems related to biology and health. For example, bioengineers might use their skills to design a prosthetic (artificial) arm or leg for someone who has lost theirs.

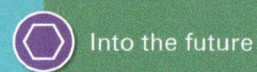 Into the future

Faster, higher, farther

Sports equipment is all designed using cutting-edge engineering and mathematical processes. For example:

Formulas **assess the texture and material** of balls to *optimize* grip or bounce.

Mathematical models are used to work out air flow around bicycle helmets.

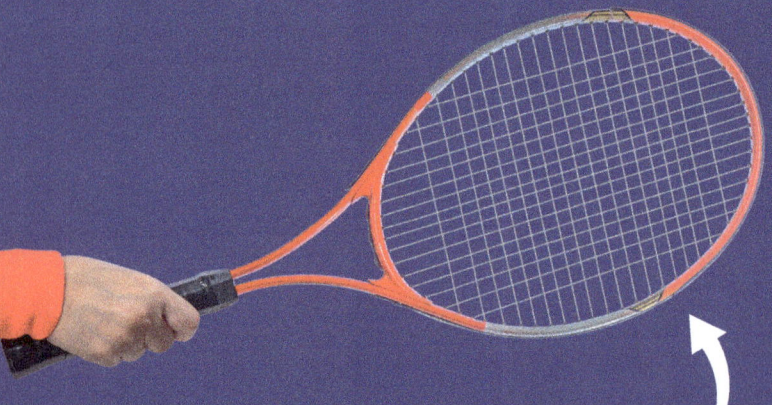

Math is used to calculate the best weight distribution and string tension in rackets.

Smart watches are like mini computers on your wrist, monitoring all your health data. Such metrics as body mass index (BMI) and body ratios, heart rates, and average speeds are all available at the touch of a button.

In the field of sports, math and technology are helping humans set themselves challenges and push themselves to their limits to be the very best they can be.

On the field, such features as VAR and goal-line technology are changing how sports are both played and refereed. The math behind them gives more accurate outcomes—although not everyone is a fan!

TECH TIME

The latest in sports safety tech are mouth guards containing tiny accelerometer chips. These measure impact during training and when athletes collide on the field. Monitoring this "contact load" helps to assess—and avoid—head injuries.

Design and make a space parachute

You will need:
- Plastic bags
- A pair of scissors
- String
- Tape
- Small objects, such as wrapped candies
- A timer or stopwatch

Give it a try

1. Cut out a circle about 8 inches across from one of the plastic bags. This is your parachute canopy.
2. Cut 8 small pieces of tape and place them evenly around the edges of the canopy.
3. Cut 8 pieces of string. Make sure they are all the same length.
4. Make holes through the tape and canopy, and thread the pieces of string through each one.
5. Either tape or tie the pieces of string to your small object (the **payload**).
6. Drop your parachute from the highest height that you can safely reach, and time how long it takes to hit the ground.

Use your math skills to design a parachute

that will drop some scientific instruments on another planet as slowly and carefully as possible.

Try this next!

How do you think you could slow the parachute down? What measurements do you need to change? Think about the size and shape of the canopy, the material the canopy was made from, the weight of your payload, and the height from which you dropped it. Repeat the experiment, changing some of these **variables** to see what combination of factors creates the safest descent.

QUESTION TIME!

What connections can you see between the different factors and measurements? What conclusions can you state about the relationship between different variables?

Index

A
AI, 36
airplanes, 20, 21
Aldrin, Buzz, 33
algebra, 7, 22, 38
algorithms, 6, 7, 8, 11, 13
Ameca, 39
Armstrong, Neil, 33

B
Babbage, Charles 10
binary math 11
bioengineering, 41
bridges, 5, 24, 25

C
car design, 18, 19
civil engineering, 24
communication, 12–13
computers, 6, 10–11

D
dams, 23, 25
data, 12, 13, 39
deep learning, 15

E
eclipses, 26, 29
encryption, 12
energy sources, 17, 22–23
equations, 7, 11, 20, 23, 25
escape velocity, 30

F
formulas, 18, 22, 25

G
Galilei, Galileo, 29
game theory, 9
geometry, 7, 8, 24
GPS, 19
gravity, 21, 23, 27, 30, 31

H
health and fitness, 37, 42–43

I
infrastructure, 17, 24–25
internet, 11, 15

K
kinematics, 38

M
machine learning, 15
Mars, 34–35
mathematical modeling, 31, 42
medicine, 36, 40–41
moon, 26, 27, 29, 32–33
Morgan, JoAnn, 33

O
optimization, 9, 18
orbital mechanics, 31, 34

P
pi, 35
Pythagoras, 25

R
ReCAPTCHA, 11
robots, 34, 35, 36, 38–39

S
satellites, 19, 31
ships, 21
smart devices, 6, 14–15, 42
social media, 13
spacecraft, 30–31, 32
sports, 42–43
statistics, 13, 14, 39

T
telescopes, 28, 29
text messages, 12
transformations, 9
transportation, 5, 16–17, 18–19, 20–21
trigonometry, 21
trilateration, 19
tunnels, 24, 25
Turing, Alan, 11

V
vectors, 21
video games, 5, 8–9, 37

W
Wald, Abraham, 20
WhatsApp, 12

Glossary

algebra (AL juh bruh)—a branch of math that uses letters and numbers to show relationships between quantities

calculus (KAL kyuh luhs)—a type of math that deals with rates of change in systems or processes

deep learning (deep LUR nihng)—a type of machine learning that uses artificial neurons (brain cells) to learn in a way similar to human learning

encryption (ehn KRIHP shuhn)—the act of turning data or information into code so other people can't read it

equation (ih KWAY zhuhn)—a mathematical statement that has two equal sides separated by an equal sign (=)

formula (FAWR myuh luh)—a set of letters or numbers that represents the information you need to know and the way to solve a math problem

geometry (jee OM uh tree)—a branch of math that measures and compares lines, angles, surfaces, and solids in space

machine learning (muh SHEEN LUR nihng)—a type of artificial intelligence (AI) where machines learn from data and improve their own performance without human input

mass (mas)—the amount of matter something contains

optimization (OP tuh muh ZAY shuhn)—the act of changing a process to make a favorable outcome more likely

payload (PAY LOHD)—a rocket's cargo, including all its passengers and instruments

probability (PROB uh BIHL uh tee)—the likelihood that an event will occur, estimated as a ratio

radius (RAY dee uhs)—the distance from the middle of a circle to its edge

statistics (stuh TIHS tihks)—a type of math that deals with collecting, presenting, and analyzing data

streamlined (STREEM LYND)—describing a shape that is designed to have the least possible resistance to air or water, so it moves smoothly and quickly

trajectory (truh JEHK tuhr ee)—a curved path, like the path a planet in orbit or a spacecraft takes

trigonometry (TRIHG uh NOM uh tree)—a type of math that deals with the relationships between the sides and angles of triangles

variable (VAIR ee uh buhl)—something that changes or that could have any one of several different values

vector (VEHK tuhr)—a measure that includes both magnitude (size) and direction

volume (VOL yuhm)—the amount of space that an object takes up

www.ingramcontent.com/pod-product-compliance
Lightning Source LLC
Chambersburg PA
CBHW061252170426
43191CB00041B/2413